Columbia University

Contributions to Education

Teachers College Series

No. 439

AMS PRESS
NEW YORK

GENERALIZATION OF BRIGHT AND DULL CHILDREN

A COMPARATIVE STUDY
WITH SPECIAL REFERENCE TO SPELLING

144234

By

HERBERT ALLEN CARROLL, Ph.D.

ASSISTANT PROFESSOR OF EDUCATIONAL PSYCHOLOGY
UNIVERSITY OF MINNESOTA

TEACHERS COLLEGE, COLUMBIA UNIVERSITY
CONTRIBUTIONS TO EDUCATION, No. 439

LB1574
C3
1972

BUREAU OF PUBLICATIONS
Teachers College, Columbia University
NEW YORK CITY
1930

Library of Congress Cataloging in Publication Data

Carroll, Herbert Allen, 1897-
   Generalization of bright and dull children.

   Reprint of the 1930 ed., issued in series: Teachers
College, Columbia University. Contributions to education, no. 439.
   Originally presented as the author's thesis, Columbia.
   Includes bibliographical references.
   1. Spelling ability. 2. Exceptional children--Edu-
cation. 3. Ability. I. Title. II. Series: Columbia University. Teachers College. Contributions
to education, no. 439.
LB1574.C3   1972   372.6'32   78-176629
ISBN 0-404-55439-3

Reprinted by Special Arrangement with Teachers
College Press, New York, New York

From the edition of 1930, New York
First AMS edition published in 1972
Manufactured in the United States

AMS PRESS, INC.
NEW YORK, N. Y.   10003

ACKNOWLEDGMENTS

I am deeply indebted to the Institute of School Experimentation, Teachers College, Columbia University, for the privilege of making this study as a part of the research program of Section D, under the immediate direction of Professor Arthur I. Gates, and the general supervision of the Director, Professor Otis W. Caldwell. Professor Gates at all times kept in close touch with the investigation, and made many valuable suggestions.

I am also appreciative of the criticisms and recommendations made by Professor L. S. Hollingworth and Professor J. R. Mc-Gaughy, and of help received from James E. Mendenhall's study of spelling errors.

The cordial coöperation of Mr. Frederick B. Graham, principal of Public School 210, Brooklyn, New York, and of his assistant, Miss Mabel Leonard, did much toward making this investigation possible.

H. A. C.

CONTENTS

CHAPTER   PAGE

I. THE PROBLEM 1
   Generalization and Transfer 1
   Generalization in Spelling 4
   Generalization and Intelligence 7

II. RELATED STUDIES 9
   The Learning of Bright and of Dull Children 9

III. GATHERING THE RAW DATA 12
   The Word List 15
   Method of Giving the Tests 16

IV. PROCEDURE IN ANALYZING MISSPELLINGS 17
   Kinds of Errors 17
   Syllables and Word Length 21
   Phonetic Analysis 22

V. RESULTS: NUMBER AND KINDS OF ERRORS 25
   Irrelevant Errors Eliminated 30
   Comparison Between the Ten Brightest and the Ten
      Dullest Children from Each Grade............. 31
   Words on Children's Grade Level 33
   Summary 36

VI. RESULTS: WORD AND SYLLABLE PLACEMENT OF ERRORS 37
   Effect of Syllable Length of Word 37
   Syllable Placement of Errors 40

VII. RESULTS: PHONETIC ANALYSIS 43

VIII. CONCLUSIONS AND IMPLICATIONS 48
   Kinds of Errors 48
   Word Length and Syllable Placement 51
   Phonetic Analysis 52
   Educational Implications 53
   Summary 54

TABLES

TABLE   PAGE

I. Composition of the Experimental Groups 14

II. Composition of Groups Made up of Children Having the Ten Highest and the Ten Lowest IQ's in Each Grade 23

III. A Comparative Analysis of the Number and Kinds of Errors 26

IV. A Comparative Analysis of Number and Kinds of Errors with All Wholly Irrelevant Misspellings Omitted 30

V. A Comparative Analysis of the Number and Kinds of Errors Made by the Ten Brightest and the Ten Dullest Children of Each Grade 32

VI. Distribution of Percentages of Irrelevant Errors of the Ten Brightest and the Ten Dullest Children of Each Grade 33

VII. A Comparative Analysis of Number and Kinds of Errors from Words on Subjects' Grade Level and in Words Given One Year in Advance 34

VIII. Comparative Percentages of Misspellings, on Basis of Syllable Length of Word by the Ten Brightest and the Ten Dullest Children from Each Grade 39

IX. Comparative Percentages of Syllable Placement of Errors Made by the Ten Brightest and the Ten Dullest Children from Each Grade 41

X. Comparative Analysis of Syllable Placement of Error in 656 Four-syllable Words 42

XI. A Comparative Phonetic Analysis 44

XII. A Comparative Phonetic Analysis of the Words Misspelled by the Ten Brightest and the Ten Dullest Children in Each Grade... 45

XIII. A Comparative Phonetic Analysis of Words Given on Subjects' Grade Level and Words Given One Year in Advance of Grade Level 47

FIGURES

FIGURE   PAGE

1. A Comparison of Distribution of Number of Errors Made by Bright
   and Dull Children 25

2. A Comparative Analysis of Kinds of Errors 29

3. Word and Syllable Frequency of Errors 38

4. Phonetic Misspellings by the Ten Brightest and the Ten Dullest Children from Each Grade 46

GENERALIZATION OF BRIGHT AND DULL CHILDREN

A COMPARATIVE STUDY
WITH SPECIAL REFERENCE TO SPELLING

CHAPTER I

THE PROBLEM

The present study was organized with the idea of uncovering through the medium of a school subject the comparative ability of bright and dull children to generalize. There are three main lines of approach to the problem: (1) through an analysis of the kinds of spelling errors made; (2) through an analysis of the syllable placement of the errors and of the incidence of errors with respect to the length of words in terms of syllables; (3) through a phonetic analysis of the misspelled words. Before the data gathered from these analyses are presented, the meaning of the term *generalization* and its application to spelling should be clearly understood.

GENERALIZATION AND TRANSFER

Dewey[1] defines *generalization* as "the process by which a principle or law is reached; the term is also used to denote the production. The term expresses the use of a function of induction, which endeavors, beginning with a number of scattered details, to arrive at a general statement. . . . Logically, a principle not only sums up and registers the net intellectual outcome of a great many different experiences which have been undergone at diverse times and places, but it is an illuminating and clarifying means of interpreting new cases that without it could not be understood."

Dewey, it will be noted, does not limit generalization to a conscious production of a law. In the same vein, Watson[2] makes the statement that "transfer may, and often does, occur in instances where no overt conscious recognition of common elements has

[1] Dewey, J., in *Cyclopedia of Education*, 1912, p. 15.
[2] Watson, A., in an unpublished doctor's dissertation, Teachers College, Columbia University.

1

been made." This is important in view of the fact that many of the supporters of the theory of *generalization*, as opposed to *transfer*, assert, as does Orata,[3] that there must be present at the time the transfer is made "a conscious adaptation of means to ends." Judd makes a great deal of such a conscious adaptation, stressing the important part played by the teacher in facilitating generalization. But the supporters of the "identical elements" theory have not overlooked this factor. In 1929 Thorndike and Gates[4] wrote, "The methods used in guiding the pupil's learning activities have marked effect upon the degree of transfer. The more clearly the crucial element or fact or principle in a situation is brought to the pupil's attention the more readily the same element or fact or principle may be identified in another situation. Transfer in many cases depends very largely upon becoming sensitive to the essential factors in an experience which were also the crucial factors in preceding experiences."

Although anything approaching an exhaustive analysis of the supposedly conflicting points of view of those who support the theory of *generalization* and of those supporting that of *transfer* is quite impossible in an investigation of this nature, a few further explanatory quotations and remarks will aid in an understanding of the use of the two terms.

Thorndike,[5,6] explains *transfer* on the basis of identical elements. He says, "To any new situation man responds as he would to some situation like it, or like some element of it." But he goes on to say, and this is one of the things that Judd and others seem to have overlooked, "Although every change must be in a specified bond . . . some of these particularized bonds are of very widespread value. . . . There are bonds involving situations and elements of situations which are, in the ordinary sense of the word, general. . . ."

Judd,[7,8] maintaining that his theory of generalization is diametrically opposed to Thorndike's conception of transfer on the basis

[3] Orata, P. T., *The Theory of Identical Elements*, p. 158. Columbus, Ohio: Ohio State University Press, 1928.
[4] Thorndike, E. L. and Gates, A. I., *Elementary Principles of Education*, p. 104. New York: Macmillan Co., 1929.
[5] Thorndike, E. L., *Educational Psychology*, Vol. II, p. 35. New York: Bureau of Publications, Teachers College, Columbia University, 1914.
[6] Thorndike, E. L., *op. cit.*, p. 418.
[7] Judd, C. H., *Psychology of Secondary Education*, p. 78. Boston: Ginn and Co., 1927.
[8] Judd, C. H., *op. cit.*, p. 417

of identical elements, argues as follows: "The same element of experience may and does appear in numerous settings. A right angle, for example, may be part of a square or part of a triangle. The mind which has learned to concentrate on the right angle in each of these settings makes the further discovery that the right angles found in the two cases have identical geometrical properties." So far, at least, Judd's theory is not at variance with Thorndike's. He goes on to say: "Human language and human thought exhibit what we call *generalization*. By this statement we indicate the fact that no experience remains in the human mind in isolated form. One never thinks of an item which is presented to one's senses without relating it to the other experiences which make up the content of one's thinking." On this point Judd has very recently been supported by Lashley,[9] who writes, "The complete isolation of functions becomes more and more questionable, until it seems as though disturbance in any function implies lesser, but recognizable changes in every other." But Thorndike[10] does not uphold the theory of the complete isolation of acts. As far back as 1914 he said, "Some careless thinkers have rushed from the belief in totally generalized training to the belief that training is totally specialized."

Continuing his argument, Judd [11] says, "In opposition to Thorndike's view, the doctrine that education is training in generalization maintains that experience is changed in quality by its organization. There is no identity of successive elements in mental experience, because experience is always a manifestation of organization. . . . It is the very nature of generalization and abstraction that they extend beyond the particular experiences in which they originate." But Thorndike has already been quoted to the effect that "there are bonds involving situations and elements of situations which are, in the ordinary sense of the word, general."

Judd fails to make himself exactly clear as to how "experience is changed in quality by its organization." Possibly he is here advancing the Gestalt view that the whole is greater than the sum of all its parts, yet he is basing *generalization* upon "particular experiences," which is analytic and therefore non-Gestalt.

[9] Lashley, K. S., "Basic Neural Mechanisms in Behavior." *Psychological Review*, January, 1930, p. 18.
[10] Thorndike, E. L., *op. cit.*, p. 365.
[11] Judd, C. H., *op. cit.*, pp. 439–441.

Looked at broadly, it is difficult to see how Judd's theory differs sharply from Thorndike's conception that, pragmatically, identical transfer becomes general in many situations. Sandiford[12] takes the stand that there is actually no difference between the two points of view. He says, "Judd's generalization of experience . . . resolves itself into nothing more nor less than the formation of specific . . . habits having applicability to situations other than those in which they were learned." And Douglass,[13] summing up the views on transfer, says, "In the minds of many psychologists a theory of transfer based upon the process of generalization is not opposed to one which conceives of transfer as occurring through identical elements. On the contrary, when sanely interpreted, the two theories are useful supplements to each other."

The conclusion to which the writer has come is that Judd and Thorndike are fundamentally one with respect to transfer, though each is emphasizing an opposite extreme. Therefore, throughout the course of this discussion the two terms, *generalization* and *transfer*, will be used interchangeably and synonymously.

GENERALIZATION IN SPELLING

Some years ago Gates [14] said, "Reading is by no means a unitary function, an ability to be learned in general." The same contention may be made in regard to spelling—it is not an ability to be learned in general. Even if it were highly desirable for the child to look upon each word as an extant entity, it is quite impossible for him to do so. His reactions to the elements involved will depend upon his associations with previous words. As Watson[15] says, "The spelling of any word is never an isolated function; it is likely to be affected either adversely or favorably by the readiness and potency of neural bonds formed in previous experiences with somewhat similar words." Horn,[16] on the same subject, writes "Since the ability to spell cannot be credited to original nature,

12 Sandiford, P., *Educational Psychology*, p. 298. New York: Longmans, Green and Co., 1928.

13 Douglass, A. A., *Secondary Education*, p. 352. Boston: Houghton Mifflin Co., 1927.

14 Gates, A. I., "A Critique of Methods of Estimating and Measuring the Transfer of Training." *Journal of Educational Psychology.* Vol. 15, 1924, p. 549.

15 Watson, A., *op. cit.*

16 Horn, E., "The Influence of Past Experiences Upon Spelling." *Journal of Educational Research*, April, 1929, p. 283.

his [the child's] present efforts must be ascribed to what he has learned about spelling in the past. For, although many of the spellings which he writes are indeed grotesque, they are not due to a mere chance selection and arrangement of letters." But this view does not lead Horn to support the use of generalization in the teaching of spelling, for he feels that such generalization is more likely to be harmful than valuable. Archer,[17] however, takes the position, which seems to be the sounder of the two, that "the child is certain to generalize in some way or other, and, since that is the case, it is the duty of psychologists to find out how to guide that generalization into the proper channels."

Regardless of what one may think with respect to the value of training in generalization in spelling, it must be constantly kept in mind that transfer, as both Horn and Archer point out, may be negative as well as positive. Archer[18] says that transfer "may result in either improvement or loss of ability to spell related words," while Horn,[19] expressing himself more emphatically, speaks of the "naive and erroneous, but very common, assumption that past experiences in spelling necessarily transfer in a desirable way in learning new words. . . ." He goes on to say, "When a child attempts to spell a word for the first time he may be led into error by the fact that the individual sounds in the word have been spelled in a variety of ways in other words which the child has already learned to spell."

The present investigation is not concerned primarily with finding out whether or not the effects of training in generalization in spelling are salutary; that is one of many problems remaining to be solved. Only the facts of the existence of generalization itself are pertinent to this study.

It is obvious that children do generalize in spelling. That being the case, it will be interesting to discover the factors which serve as bases for their generalizations.

Generalization, by its very nature, as was brought out in the discussion given earlier in this chapter, requires analysis. It never goes on when the thing observed is considered as a whole. Hence there can be no generalization in the spelling of a word

[17] Archer, C. P., "Saving Time in Spelling Instruction." *Journal of Educational Research*, September, 1929, p. 131.
[18] Archer, C. P., *op. cit.*, p. 122.
[19] Horn, E., *op. cit.*, p. 282.

unless that word is divided into parts, or unless, perhaps, as in the case of phonetic transfer in dealing with a monosyllable, the word is looked upon as a single sound.

With respect to spelling there may be said to be three types of possible generalization: the visual, the motor, and the phonetic types. In visual generalization, the child observes the configuration of the word—its length, and its appearance or shape. For example, he has quite a different picture when he thinks of such a word as *cat* from that which he has when he thinks of *automobile*. To write *automobile* with as few as three letters would be an unlikely act for a child who could generalize well. He would see immediately that in the matter of length the word *automobile* and the spelling *aum*, let us say, are not identical. Hence the visual picture of the length of a word is a basis for transfer.

A factor which is perhaps not quite so important is the shape of the word. *Coffee*, for example, has a different appearance from the word *secure*. If the two *f*'s, rising above the line, have caught the child's attention, he is not likely to spell the word in letters that all fall below the line or are even with it. This is a good example of an instance where the transfer might easily be made unconsciously.

In addition to the configuration of the word as a whole, the visual elements of its parts often serve as bases for transfer. In a long word, such as *unnecessary*, the child may make a syllable approach, in which case each syllable presents certain visual characteristics which aid him in the spelling of the word. He will remember, perhaps, that *un* is short, and that its letters are of average height. All these elements aid him in his spelling.

Besides containing certain visual elements which serve as bases for transfer, words possess a motor character—rhythm and pronunciation units. The child catches the motor rhythm of the word through practice in writing it, a fact, by the way, which almost completely eliminates this type of transfer from consideration in this study, since, presumably, the children who were the subjects of the tests given were writing for the first time the words given in the preliminary test. The number of pronunciation units, however, remains as a possible element of transfer for the subjects of this study. That is, if the child were given the word *nevertheless*, he would note that it has four parts. Therefore, for a child to spell the word with three letters, such as *nep*, would show a complete lack of this type of motor transfer; but to spell it *nepirdoning* would show that the number of pronunciation units, at least, had been carried over to the actual spelling of the word. Because of the technique used in this investigation, the phonetic qualities of the word are more likely bases for transfer than is either of the two elements previously discussed. When a child spells a word phonetically, he manifests an ability to translate sound into letters. If he spell *limb* as *lim*, who is there to say that he is not logically justified? In making phonetic transfers, the child may consider the word as a whole—if it is a short one—or he may consider the sound qualities of the syllables or of any letter combinations which make up phonograms, or phonetic units. Very often, perhaps most often, he considers single letters. Tidyman[20] says that "one-fifth of the errors that children make are due to the confusion of vowels having obscure or equivalent sounds." In substituting one vowel for another of equivalent sound the child is making a perfectly good transfer; he is simply unfortunate if in this instance it happens to be negative.

In this study all phonetic analysis has been made on a letter basis, as it would be unfair to penalize the child for failing to realize that certain letters, such as final "e," have in many specific instances, altered the sound of a preceding letter.

GENERALIZATION AND INTELLIGENCE

"One of the most important forms of the thought process is that of drawing and using generalizations, the process of seeing relationships, and of using these statements of relationship in the solution of problems," says Billings.[21] Since it appears even to superficial observation that the intelligent see relationships more quickly than the less intelligent, one immediately begins to wonder if the bright generalize more than the dull. It is with this problem—the relationship of generalization-ability and intelligence—that this study is primarily concerned.

In one of his investigations of spelling, Archer[22] came to the conclusion that "intelligence as here tested does not appear to be

---

[20] Tidyman, W. F., *The Teaching of Spelling*, p. 56. Yonkers, N. Y.: World Book Co., 1926.
[21] Billings, N., *Generalizations Basic to the Social Studies Curriculum*, p. 17. Baltimore: Warwick & York, 1929.
[22] Archer, C. P., *op. cit.*, p. 129.

a factor" in the amount of transfer made. Brooks,[23] in a study of the relation of transfer to intelligence, concludes, "In this investigation Mental Age and IQ are found in most tests to bear a low positive or negative (really neutral) relation to residual gains or transfer." On the other hand, Thorndike and Gates[24] say, "The native ability of a pupil has a pronounced effect upon the degree of transfer. In most subjects, the brighter pupils, other things being equal, can make wider use of their acquisition than duller pupils. Brightness, indeed, means in a considerable measure sensitivity to the factors or principles which are common to many situations. Not only do the bright pupils isolate the essential elements in a learning situation more quickly, but they also perceive more acutely the same elements in new settings. Transfer of experience therefore occurs more fully among bright than among dull individuals; it is in considerable degree determined by intelligence."

In his classic study of mental discipline in high school, Thorndike came to conclusions which probably prompted the above statement. From careful experimental work with 8,564 students from Grades IX, X, and XI, he discovered that a study is not valuable in itself because it develops ability to transfer, but that abler pupils, taking certain subjects, cause those subjects to appear to have a great transfer value. In other words, to quote Thorndike[25] exactly, "Whatever studies they [the bright] take will seem to produce large gains in intellect," because of the fact that "those who have the most to begin with gain the most during the year" irrespective of subject material.

The present investigation, as stated in the opening paragraph, aims to determine whether or not bright pupils generalize more than dull pupils in the field of spelling. Keeping in mind the elements which serve as bases for such generalization, the attempt will be made to discover what form or forms of transfer are most widely used, and how the two groups differ in such use. Besides being of theoretical value, the findings should be suggestive in the practical field of teaching procedure used with differentiated classes.

[23] Brooks, F. D., "The Transfer of Training in Relation to Intellect." *Journal of Educational Research*, Vol. 15, 1924, p. 422.
[24] Thorndike, E. L. and Gates, A. I., *op. cit.*, p. 104.
[25] Thorndike, E. L., "Mental Discipline in High School Studies." *Journal of Educational Psychology*, Vol. 15, 1924, p. 95.

CHAPTER II

RELATED STUDIES

As far as the writer has been able to discover, there has been no comparative study whatever of the effect of intelligence upon generalization in a specific school subject. However, statements from investigations of the learning of bright and dull children will aid toward a better understanding of the special problems with which this experiment is concerned.

THE LEARNING OF BRIGHT AND OF DULL CHILDREN

In 1906 Terman,[1] already deeply interested in atypical children, reported a study made by him of seven bright and seven dull boys. "Group I [the bright group] is superior to Group II [the dull group] in all the mental tests and inferior in the motor tests. . . . All of the subjects were asked whether they preferred to read or to play games. With the exception of E, who gave an uncertain answer, all of Group I replied that they preferred reading. Every subject of Group II preferred games. . . . The study has strengthened my impression of the relatively greater importance of endowment over training as a determinant of an individual's intellectual rank among his fellows." It is interesting to note that Terman has continued through the years to hold to the view just stated with respect to endowment.

In 1926 Brown[2] made a study of the unevenness of the abilities of dull and bright children. He says as his final word, "The only conclusions which it seems possible to arrive at logically are that dull boys and bright boys show an equal amount of unevenness in all the abilities considered here; that the abilities of one group are as highly specialized or different as the abilities of another; and that, as far as this specialization is a determining factor, the two groups should have the same type of class organization and treatment. Each boy of each group should be considered a unique

[1] Terman, L. M., "Genius and Stupidity." *Pedagogical Seminary*, Vol. 13, 1906, p. 372.
[2] Brown, A. W., *The Unevenness of the Abilities of Dull and Bright Children*, p. 109. New York: Bureau of Publications, Teachers College, Columbia University, 1926.

9

individual who needs individual education and vocational guidance." This finding would seem to militate against the desirability of differentiating classes on the basis of intelligence tests, if not within the subject itself. In other words, Brown finds such specificity of abilities that grouping pupils through the medium of an intelligence test appears to him to be impracticable.

Directly in agreement with Brown's conclusions is the statement of Pyle and Snadden [3] that "if the brightest and most successful high school pupils are compared with the dullest and least successful pupils, it is found that in some types of work, including certain forms of learning, some members of the dull group will excel some members of the bright group."

Overlapping of ability groups appears to be inevitable. Further substantiating the position just given are the conclusions reached by Wilson [4] in his study of the *Learning of Bright and Dull Children.* He says: "It [the study] presents evidence that, on the average, selection of children by the Binet test (1) fairly well assures the quality of performance on certain tasks requiring responses of like character, viz, largely mental; and (2) gives less and less assurance of the quality of performance on other tasks requiring greater and greater proportions of gross muscular responses. It further presents evidence that, for individuals, selection by the Binet test gives only slight assurance of the quality of performance on any kind of task, but, in work involving a greater proportion of gross muscular movement, the prediction is more uncertain than in work that is largely mental. . . . There does not seem to be any ability to learn in the sense of a common factor. Difference in ability to learn various responses are different in degree, not in kind. But so many functions are involved in the practical experiences of life that for these groups, separated in age by three years and in brightness by 30 IQ points, *ability to learn in general is characterized for all practical purposes by difference in kind.** Brighter individuals have that kind of ability which makes economical progress in work requiring a small proportion of gross motor movement. Dull individuals have that

* Italics are the author's.

[3] Pyle, W. H. and Snadden, G. H., "An Experimental Study of Bright and Dull High School Pupils." *Journal of Educational Psychology*, April, 1929, p. 268.

[4] Wilson, F. T., *Learning of Bright and Dull Children*, pp. 48–49. New York: Bureau of Publications, Teachers College, Columbia University, 1928.

kind of ability which makes economical progress in work requiring a large proportion of gross muscular movement." Wilson's statement with regard to the comparative ability of the bright and dull in mental and muscular functions agrees very closely with the findings of Terman, previously quoted.

Huber [5] in her study, which is similar in some respects to the one which the writer is undertaking, attempted to discover the influence of intelligence upon children's reading. The subjects of her experiment comprised fifteen classes in five public schools of Yonkers, New York. She worked with three groups of children: a dull, an average, and a bright group. The dull group had a mean IQ of 74.4; the average group, 98.5; the bright group, 114.6. She came to two conclusions: "(1) Children at all levels of intelligence are appreciative of the quality of reading material. Dull children, as well as those more fortunately endowed in intelligence, appreciate the merit of stories and poems which are offered them. (2) A factor of importance in arranging courses of study in reading is complexity of material. It is necessary that material be graded carefully to the pupil's level of intelligence. Bright children can appreciate material of a wide range of difficulty, but in preparing reading material for dull children care should be taken to avoid unusual words, confused or involved sentence and paragraph structure, or abstract and subtle ideas." This conclusion coincides with Baker's [6] statement: "In dealing with mental difference from this point of view, we find that a low IQ signifies a pupil who must have material presented in short and simple units, with immediate ends, whereas a high IQ signifies the need of large units of a comprehensive nature, which have very ulterior ends. The low IQ denotes work of concrete nature, whereas the high IQ denotes work of an abstract, generalized, and complicated nature." The findings of Huber and Baker give some support to the idea that bright children do generalize more than the dull.

Although differences were found between bright and dull children in each of the investigations just presented, in no case were they strikingly large. Therefore, the recommendations of the investigators are moderate.

[5] Huber, M. B., *The Influence of Intelligence upon Children's Reading Interests*, p. 39. New York: Bureau of Publications, Teachers College, Columbia University, 1928.
[6] Baker, H. J., *Characteristic Differences in Bright and Dull Pupils*, p. 4. Bloomington, Ill.; Public School Publishing Company, 1927.

CHAPTER III

GATHERING THE RAW DATA

The raw data used in this experiment were gathered in Public School 210, Brooklyn, New York. This school, with an enrollment of about 2,700, is in a section of the city which is predominantly Jewish.

It was desirable, for the purposes of this investigation, to choose subjects from Grades IV and V. The causes of misspellings by children in the grades lower than Grade IV are difficult to determine, such a factor as handwriting, for example, often resulting in the appearance of errors even though the child actually knows how to spell the words. The higher grades were not chosen, for it becomes increasingly difficult to present a novel situation to children as they grow older, because of the length and varied nature of their previous training. Grades IV and V, then, were thought to be the best for the experiment.

In Grade IV, both groups A and B (A representing the less advanced half) were chosen. In Grade V it was necessary to omit A, since it was made up of but two sections and hence offered neither a preëminently dull nor a preëminently bright group. B, however, presented no such difficulties. In IV A there were five sections, in IV B four sections, and in V B four sections. In each of these three grades the brightest and the dullest sections were chosen for the purpose of this experiment. These classes had already been very carefully differentiated on the basis of the following plan, worked out in great detail at Public School 210.

On entering Public School 210, the procedure is that I A children are graded by means of the Pintner-Cunningham Intelligence Tests. At the end of I B they are retested, this time with Haggerty Delta I, and they are regraded on the basis of the test results combined with the teacher's judgment. At the end of II B, they are regrouped, this time on the basis of the teacher's judgment and the result of the Otis Primary Intelligence Test.

A year later, at the end of III B, children are again classified and

12

graded. This time the results of an achievement test—usually the Stanford Test—are utilized. The Mental Age, the Educational Age, and the Pedagogical Age are then averaged, resulting in a Promotion Age. To get an index of a child's brightness, the Promotion Age is divided by the Chronological Age, giving a Promotion Quotient, on which figure grades are sectioned. Cards are arranged by Promotion Quotients and classes cut off, the size and number of such classes being dependent upon the administrative policy of the school.

Such a procedure helps to explain why there is some overlapping of IQ's in the sections studied in this investigation.

Unfortunately, it was impossible for the writer to give Stanford-Binet Tests to the two hundred children serving as subjects in this experiment. It therefore became necessary to accept the IQ's found from group tests administered at the school.

In order to get a more exact measure than that represented by the score on a single test, the last two IQ's found for the child were averaged and the result was set down as the index to the individual's mental ability. When the quotient was a fraction, the nearest even number was accepted. That is, if the average was found to be 87.5, the child's IQ was said to be 88; if 86.5, 86, etc.

The intelligence tests from which IQ's had been found for the children who were now in IV A and IV B were the Otis Primary and the Haggerty Delta II tests; in V B, the tests used were the Haggerty Delta II and the National Intelligence Test. There were but two exceptions—two instances where the Stanford-Binet Test had been given. In the cases of forty-nine children, but one IQ was available.

It was found, on treating the intelligence ratings of the groups chosen, that the mean IQ of the three bright groups was 124.9, with a standard deviation of 16.3. The mean IQ of the three dull groups was 92.0, with a standard deviation of 12.9. The objection may immediately be made that, according to Terman's classification, although the bright group is really bright, the dull group is not dull; that is, 124.9 unquestionably places the so-called bright group with very superior children, while the 92.0 average makes the dull group belong with the low normal group. However, the writer wishes to make it clear that the problems considered in this study are educational ones, and that to deal with the highest and the lowest section of each class is of more practical value than to deal solely with the children having the highest and the lowest IQ's. An actual school situation, not a hypothetical one, is undergoing analysis.

It should, then, be kept in mind throughout the course of this study that whenever the word *bright* is used the writer is referring to the brightest section or sections; whenever the word *dull* is used, the reference is to the dullest section or sections. The terms are comparative rather than scientifically exact. It will be noted that there is a difference of 32.9 between the mean IQ's of the two main groups.

The total number of children in the three bright sections was originally 114; in the three dull sections, 116. It was found on looking up the records, that certain important data—in most cases the IQ's—were lacking for sixteen of the dull, leaving 100 dull children for whom data were complete. There was a similar lack of information for nine of the bright children, leaving 105 bright children with complete data. In order to facilitate calculations, as well as to have the groups exactly equated as to

TABLE I

COMPOSITION OF THE EXPERIMENTAL GROUPS

CLASS	N	MEAN IQ	σ	RANGE IN IQ
IV A				
Bright	36	126.4	8.8	101–148
Dull	36	88.5	9.8	66–109
IV B				
Bright	35	110.5	11.3	90–148
Dull	25	89.5	13.7	59–122
V B				
Bright	29	140.6	12.3	120–168
Dull	39	96.8	11.2	66–131
TOTAL				
Bright	100	124.9 ± 1.09	16.3	90–168
Dull	100	92.0 ± .87	12.9	59–131

number, it was decided to eliminate five more of the children of the bright group, leaving 100. The five children eliminated were members of V B, the records of every seventh child being discarded in order to be sure of a random elimination. (See Table I* for further details with respect to the composition of the two groups.)

THE WORD LIST

The words chosen for the purposes of this experiment were taken from the list made by Gates. Gates consulted several compilations of the most frequently used words, such as Ayres-Buckingham, Horn Basic Vocabulary, Gates Primary, and Thorndike lists. Having made a composite list from these, he turned next to the most popular modern spellers in order to discover the grade placement of such words. The spellers used were the following:

1. Horn-Ashbaugh, "Fundamentals of Spelling."
2. Lippincott's New Horn-Ashbaugh Speller.
3. The New York City List.
4. Jones's "Complete Course in Spelling."
5. The McCall Speller.
6. The Smith-Bagley Master Speller.
7. The Breed-French Speller.

He now had a list for all the grades, composed of words most often used by children and placed in those grades where, according to the composite opinion of authors of popular spellers, they belonged.

In order to present to the children in the present experiment a situation which was, at least comparatively, novel, words were given one year in advance of their present grade status; that is, V A words were given to IV A pupils, V B words to IV B pupils, and VI B words to V B pupils. A reason other than novelty was also considered in doing this. To get enough misspellings for experimental purposes, it was necessary to give words considerably in advance of the child's grade placement. This was especially necessary in the case of the bright children. However, in order to meet the objection that the result of the study would have been

---

* Throughout this report a minus sign will be used to indicate that the dull rate less than the bright; a plus sign to indicate that they rate more.

quite different had the children been asked to spell words adapted to their own grade level, it was decided to give a sampling of 100 words adapted to their grade level to ten children selected at random from each of the six sections. This sample was not given until February, 1930, a half year having elapsed since the main list had been given in September, 1929. The IV A children had now become IV B children; the IV B children had become V A children; and the V B children had become VI A children. However, since they had all advanced only a half year, the words given them on their own grade level were not the same ones which in September had been given to them one year in advance of their grade level. A comparison of the analysis of the two tests will be presented later.

METHOD OF GIVING THE TESTS

The method of dictating both sets of words was exactly the same. In the main test, 318 words were dictated to IV A, 320 to IV B, and 318 to V B. In the second test, 100 words, chosen at random, were given to ten children selected from each of the sections chosen for the study. With respect to the actual presentation of the words to the children, the following facts are pertinent. Fifty words were given at each sitting, the children meeting for this work once in the morning and once in the afternoon. It required, then, three and one half days to give the main list. Each teacher dictated the same set of words; that is, the words were so distributed that, after one teacher had dictated a set of fifty words to a bright group, the same teacher dictated the same set of fifty words to a dull group. This equated the teacher factor of the problem in so far as the presentation of the words was concerned. The teacher first pronounced the word; then used it in a sentence; and then pronounced it again, after which it was written by the children.

CHAPTER IV

PROCEDURE IN ANALYZING MISSPELLINGS

Approximately 68,000 words which children themselves had actually spelled were now ready to be examined. First, the entire number were examined, the misspelled words being checked. An error involving an apostrophe, a hyphen, or a capital letter was not considered as affecting the correctness of the spelling of the word. The next step was to copy the misspellings of each of the words dictated; that is, when the word *automobile* was given, all of the different ways in which the children misspelled that word were listed. Each child having previously been given a number in order that individual records as well as group records might be kept, the key number of the child who had committed the error was now placed after each listed misspelling.

KINDS OF ERRORS

After the copying of the misspellings had been completed, it became necessary to classify the errors. There are a great many classifications possible in an investigation of this kind. The writer finally decided to use a system comparable in many respects to that utilized by James Mendenhall in his dissertation, *An Analysis of Spelling Errors*.[1]

This classification is a rather rigid one, but it covers every possible error which children might make, although, as has been said before, it would have been possible to group such errors in a different fashion. Before the work of classification had proceeded very far, it became obvious that certain definite and, in many cases, arbitrary criteria would have to be set up if those analyzing the words were to be consistent both with themselves and with one another. The criteria adopted in every case grew out of actual problems arising in connection with the work of analysis. They cover every instance wherein doubt arose in the minds of the an-

[1] Mendenhall, James. An Analysis of Spelling Errors. (A Lincoln School Publication) Bureau of Publications, Teachers College, Columbia University, 1930.

alyzers as to just where to place the error, and such doubts were rather frequent. The following set of rules, adopted for the final classification, were adhered to rigidly by the three people[2] who analyzed the 34,000 spelling errors which appeared in the raw material.

Rules Governing Analysis of Misspelled Words

1. When two incorrect substitutions of letters appear in succession, the error is analyzed as a single one and placed under *groups.*
2. When two letters such as *uy* for *ye* in *rye* are substituted, the error is analyzed as: adding of *u* and omission of *e.*
3. A word is put into the column headed *Substitution of actual word* only when that actual word is very unlike the one in question. Otherwise it is analyzed, even though it is an actual word.
4. A word is put into the column headed *Substitution of an entirely irrelevant word* only when it has little or no structural relationship with the word in question. Otherwise that group of letters which is irrelevant is underlined, and the word is placed in the column headed *Substitution of a group of letters.*
5. The omission of two or more letters in succession is considered as the omission of a group of letters and looked upon as a single error.
6. Letters are said to be transposed only when they appear in succession as in *laem* for *lame.* Transposition of syllables is not considered as an error to be included in this class.
7. When a letter is added to or omitted after a transposed set of letters, it is said to be added to or omitted after the second letter as it appears in the correct spelling of the word. Example: fa*ri*ely, *ri* is transposed, *e* is a vowel added to the consonant *r.*
8. When a single letter is substituted for a group of letters, or a group of letters for a single letter, the error is considered as a single one, and placed under groups.
9. A maximum of three errors in a single word will be analyzed.
10. No specific error will be entered more than once.
11. Each specific error will be entered separately.

There is a possibility that some objections to the above set of rules may be made on the basis that they allow too many opportunities for a subjective judgment to enter into decisions with respect to irrelevant spellings. In order that the reader may see for himself exactly what was considered an irrelevant spelling of a specific word, a list of all of the wholly irrelevant words found in the spelling of the IV B dull group follows:

[2] The entire analysis was done by the author with the assistance of Miss Harryette Creasy, a graduate student in English at Columbia University, and Miss Elizabeth Price, a graduate student in Psychology at Columbia University.

Word Dictated	Irrelevant Misspelling	Word Dictated	Irrelevant Misspelling
bury	breoung	surprise	stressed
	brem		spiosise
	irey	radio	rowa
	baeve	reason	rend
		oatmeal	ouiten
fancy	fisded		onelld
	focle	reasons	rencre
		office	afa
itself	ithsfe	reduce	recirle
		tangle	talnd
butcher	buitcuse	orders	ado
	broust	tenth	tllnd
	buort	outfit	ateoy
		throat	fatel
job	gogey	palm	hoin
	driven	parade	hira
			biary
join	fuilt	parties	batteray
	quren	rush	racedl
	qolin	trouble	luupplee
		savage	sfiddish
calm	coven	umbrella	ananl
	angon		ountrely
			abler
jolly	pledl	score	caca
judge	jack	perhaps	phadle
lately	filty	view	vbedl
flutter	fotidii	deserve	dreves
follows	flaol	already	arlr
	fowolis	difference	drifle
charm	cande	guide	dyd
cheaper	shelfer	animal	onled
copper	pap	handkerchief	huacept
crops	kiks		hinscure
	poricks	earlier	herer
gentle	yate	eighteen	pent
geography	grayley	history	hdlc
	grufige	example	eacker
meadow	morrood	interesting	tutest
	node	invited	enfart
prince	peend	island	leang
prison	pranant	pleasure	oot
squeeze	sewig	voyage	vigured
	ecresce		rader

Word Dictated	Irrelevant Misspelling	Word Dictated	Irrelevant Misspelling
nation	manoise		valled
nature	metajorr	pledge	ead
poison	baad	preach	kroke
several	segei	shove	cofd
powder	parace	worn	uoomed
whether	cwaoth		

After the analysis had been completed, it seemed best, in order to make the findings of this study more clear, to combine certain of the groups. The preliminary classification was as follows:

Errors of Addition
- Consonant to Consonant { Doubling / Others
- Vowel to Vowel { Doubling / Others
- Consonant to Vowel
- Vowel to Consonant
- Groups { Syllables / Others

Errors of Omission
- Consonant after Consonant { 2nd of Double / Others
- Vowel after Vowel { 2nd of Double / Others
- Consonant after Vowel
- Vowel after Consonant
- Groups { Syllables / Others

Errors of Substitution
- Single Letters { Consonant for Consonant / Vowel for Vowel / Consonant for Vowel / Vowel for Consonant
- Group of Letters { Syllables / Others { Phonetic / Irrelevant
- Entire Word { Actual Word / Irrelevant
- Transposition

The author found that the above classification was so elaborate and detailed that it tended to blur the differences present in the work of the two groups of children. Therefore, a more compact presentation of the kinds of spelling errors was evolved as follows:

% of Errors of Addition   Single Letters { Doubling / Others   Groups

% of Errors of Omission   Single Letters { Doubling / Others   Groups

% of Errors of Substitution   Single Letters   Groups   Entire Word { Actual Word / Irrelevant   Transposition

SYLLABLES AND WORD LENGTH

The second phase of the problem, as was stated in Chapter I, has to do with the syllable placement of the error and the incidence of such errors with respect to the syllable length of the word. This task required but few criteria as there was nothing to do, in so far as the syllable length of the word was concerned, but to count the number of times that the children misspelled a one-syllable word, a two-syllable word, a three-syllable word, or a four-syllable word. As for the question of deciding in what syllable a certain error appeared, the following short set of rules was worked out progressively as the analysis presented problems to be solved.

Rules Governing Analysis of Syllable Placement of Error

1. Where one letter of a double consonant or a double vowel is omitted at the connecting point between two syllables, the error is said to be in the second of the double. Therefore, the second syllable is incorrect. Example: *open—ess.* The error is placed in the last syllable.
2. The omission of a syllable constitutes an error.
3. When a syllable is added, the error is placed in the syllable immediately preceding. Example: ath*er*lete. The error is placed in the syllable, *ath.*
4. When a letter at the connecting point between two syllables is incorrectly doubled, the error is said to be in the first of the two syllables affected. Example: ad*d*vise. The error is in the first syllable; *vise* is correct.

PHONETIC ANALYSIS

The third and most important line of attack on the problem was the classification of all the errors in the misspelled words into two groups: phonetic and non-phonetic errors. This division was made on the basis of letter phonetics. In making such a division it became obvious that subjective judgment would inevitably be a factor. Many of the misspellings were very difficult to analyze. However, it should be borne in mind that this study is primarily concerned with differences between bright and dull children; hence, if errors have been made in handling the material, they have been compensatory in the sense that neither group benefited at the expense of the other.

In order to make such a subjective influence as infinitesimal a factor as possible, a set of rules was drawn up for the experimenter to follow.

Rules Governing Phonetic Analysis

1. Wherever *e* appears it may either have an *e* sound or be silent.
2. *i* substituted for long *e* sound is phonetic.
3. *f* is always accepted as phonetic for *v*. Example: fe*f*er.
4. *t* is not phonetic for *d*. Exception: when used as a final letter, as in pas*t* for pas*sed*.
5. *k* is not phonetic for *t*.
6. *l* is called silent when it appears in words which bear a close resemblance to those words in which l is silent, such as *could* and *calf*. Example: stu*l*dent.
7. *tre* is not accepted as phonetic for *ter* unless it appears as the final syllable of the word.
8. *qo* is not phonetic for *quo*. Example: *quotation*.
9. *ei* and *ie* may be interchanged.
10. If the second of a double is dropped, the sound remains phonetic.
11. A word is declared phonetic on the basis of its sound as a whole; that is, if any part is spelled non-phonetically, it is placed in the non-phonetic group.

In order to give further assurance that when these rules were followed by two separate individuals the results of the classification of misspelled words into phonetic and non-phonetic groups would be similar, two correlations were run. The two judges in this instance were the author and the previously mentioned Miss Creasey. They classified 808 words, misspelled by twenty-one children who had been selected at random. As a result of this double checking, it was found that one judge placed 328 words in the phonetic group and 480 in the non-phonetic group, while the second judge put 338 words in the phonetic group and 470 in the non-phonetic group—a difference of only ten. In order to see how the individuals in the groups fared at the hands of the two judges, a correlation was run with the following results:

Phonetic r = .990 ±.0029

Non-phonetic r = .997 ± .00088

Whenever there was doubt as to whether or not the misspelling of a word was phonetic, the possible sounds of the letter or letters concerned were looked up in Webster's Dictionary.

The three preceding classifications included all of the words spelled by the entire number of children—100 dull children and 100 bright children. In order to make further comparisons, certain other groupings were made. First, since the objection might be made that the irrelevant spellings of the dull seriously affected the percentages in other types of errors, such irrelevant spellings were

TABLE II

COMPOSITION OF GROUPS MADE UP OF CHILDREN HAVING THE TEN HIGHEST
AND THE TEN LOWEST I.Q.'s IN EACH GRADE

CLASS	N	MEAN IQ	σ	RANGE IN IQ
IV A				
Bright	10	135.8	4.6	131–148
Dull	10	77.6	5.6	66– 84
IV B				
Bright	10	123.6	8.7	118–148
Dull	10	76.7	6.9	59– 86
V B				
Bright	10	153.9	8.3	144–168
Dull	10	81.8	6.8	66– 88
TOTAL				
Bright	30	137.8 ± 1.78	14.5	118–168
Dull	30	78.7 ± .80	6.5	59– 88

eliminated and comparisons were then made on the basis of the remaining words. Second, the ten brightest in each of the three bright sections and the ten dullest in each of the three dull sections were separated from the groups and their records were compared. (See Table II.)

In Chapter III mention was made of the fact that a sampling of words was given to a few of the children on their own grade level. The results of this sampling were analyzed in the same way as were the words of the main lists; that is, the procedure described in this chapter was followed.

CHAPTER V

RESULTS: NUMBER AND KINDS OF ERRORS

Upon correcting the 62,431 words spelled by the children in the main test given in September, 1929, it was found, as might be expected, that the dull had met with considerably more difficulty than the bright. One hundred dull children, spelling approximately the same number of words attempted by a group of bright children of an equal number, made over three times as many errors; or, putting it in a different way, while the bright misspelled but 18.9 per cent of the words which were one year in advance of their present grade status, the dull misspelled 59.8 per cent. (See Table III.)

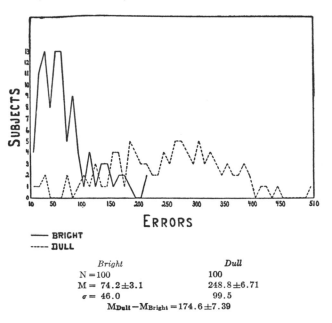

—— BRIGHT
----- DULL

Bright	Dull
N = 100	100
M = 74.2±3.1	248.8±6.71
σ = 46.0	99.5
$M_{Dull} - M_{Bright} = 174.6 \pm 7.39$	

FIG. 1. A Comparison of Distribution of Number of Errors by Bright and Dull Children

25

TABLE

A COMPARATIVE ANALYSIS OF THE

SUBJECTS	No. OF SUB- JECTS	MEAN IQ	σ	WORDS OMITTED		TOTAL WORDS SPELLED		
				Child Absent	Spelling Not At- tempted	No.	% Correct	% In- correct
IV A								
Bright	36	126.4	8.8	0	13	11,435	74.9	25.1
Dull	36	88.5	9.8	0	334	11,114	17.6	82.4
Difference		−37.9		0	+321	− 321	−57.3	+57.3
IV B								
Bright	35	110.5	11.3	100	8	11,092	79.1	20.9
Dull	25	89.5	13.7	21	10	7,969	23.2	76.8
Difference		− 21.0		− 79	+ 2	−3,123	−55.9	+55.9
V B								
Bright	29	140.6	12.3	50	24	9,148	78.7	21.3
Dull	39	96.8	11.2	650	79	11,673	17.8	82.2
Difference		− 43.8		+600	+ 55	+2,525	−60.9	+60.9
Total								
Bright	100	124.9 ± 1.09	16.3	150	45	31,675	81.1 ± .148	18.9 ± .148
Dull	100	92.0 ± .87	12.9	671	423	30,756	40.2 ± .189	59.8 ± .189
Difference		− 32.9 ± 1.40		+521	+378	− 919	+40.9 ± .240	+40.9 ± .240

It is a known fact that in differentiated sections of classes there is considerable overlapping of achievement. In order to discover whether such overlapping existed in the present instance, a comparative distribution of the number of errors made by the bright and the dull children was made. (See Figure 1.) It will be readily observed upon glancing at Figure 1 that while the two minus extremes coincide, there is a considerable difference between the two plus extremes. The largest number of errors made by a bright child proves to be 215, while the mean of the dull group is well beyond that point, and the extreme plus limit of this group goes as high as 505.

III

NUMBER AND KINDS OF ERRORS

% of Errors of Addition			% of Errors of Omission			% of Errors of Substitution					Total No. of Errors
Single Letters		Groups	Single Letters		Groups	Single Letters	Groups	Entire Word		Transposition	
Doubling	Others		Doubling	Others				Actual Word	Irrelevant		
3.4	13.3	0.6	4.6	26.7	2.9	24.3	15.0	1.4	1.6	6.3	2,871
1.9	9.5	0.7	3.3	19.0	4.5	21.0	20.3	3.5	13.9	2.5	9,163
−1.5	−3.8	+0.1	−1.3	−7.7	+2.4	−3.3	+5.3	+2.1	+12.3	−3.8	+ 6,292
2.4	15.7	1.3	7.6	27.4	3.2	21.0	14.4	0.2	0.3	6.7	2,324
1.0	14.8	1.8	3.4	24.2	5.6	22.4	21.3	0.2	1.7	3.7	6,121
−1.4	−0.9	+0.5	−4.2	−3.2	+2.4	+1.4	+6.9	0	+ 1.4	−3.0	+ 3,797
3.1	15.6	1.0	6.6	25.5	1.5	29.3	12.9	0.1	0.4	4.1	1,951
1.3	15.3	1.8	3.4	19.9	5.5	23.2	21.0	0.4	4.6	3.7	9,598
−1.8	−0.3	+0.8	−3.2	−5.6	+4.0	−6.1	+8.1	+0.3	+ 4.2	−0.4	+ 7,647
3.0	14.6	1.0	6.1	26.6	2.6	24.6	14.2	0.6	0.8	5.8	7,416
± .133	± .276	± .077	± .187	± .368	± .124	± .337	± .274	± .006	± .069	± .183	
1.5	13.1	1.4	3.4	20.7	5.2	22.3	21.0	1.5	7.3	3.3	24,882
± .052	± .143	± .049	± .077	± .172	± .095	± .178	± .174	± .052	± .111	± .076	
−1.5	−1.5	+0.4	−2.7	−5.9	+2.6	−2.3	+6.8	+0.9	+ 6.5	−2.5	+17,466
± .142	± .311	± .091	± .202	± .406	± .156	± .381	± .325	± .052	± .131	± .198	

There are other data of interest in Table III which may be considered briefly before the analysis of the kinds of errors is approached. It will be seen from Table III that the dull were much more likely to be absent than the bright. The causes for such absences were not determined. A factor of greater interest to us in the present study is the matter of children's not attempting the spelling of a word. The dull were nearly ten times as remiss as the bright in this respect. The bright, in the face of the difficult situation resulting from being asked to spell an unfamiliar word, are much more likely than the dull to courageously accept the challenge.

The differences in kinds of errors made are important. It should be kept in mind that, in arriving at the conclusions presented in Table III, over 32,000 errors were classified in eleven groups. This large number represents a considerable sampling. A study of the table brings to our attention the fact that in each of the classifications a significant difference between bright and dull is found, accepting as statistically significant a critical ratio of three or more. In some types of errors the bright exceed the dull; in others the dull exceed the bright. The bright make a higher percentage of errors in the following instances:

1. Addition of a single letter through doubling.
2. Addition of single letters which do not involve doubling.
3. Omission of the second letter of a double.
4. Omission of a single letter not one of the pair.
5. Substitution of one letter for another.
6. Transposing letters.

The dull excel the bright in the following types of errors:

1. Addition of a group of letters.
2. Omission of a group of letters.
3. Substitution of a group of letters.
4. Substitution of an entire actual word.
5. Substitution of a wholly irrelevant word.

A rather striking fact emerges from this summary of the differences; namely, that the dull are more likely to make an error involving a large part of the word; that is, they are more likely to add, omit, or substitute a group of letters. The bright, on the other hand, appear to have the greater difficulty, speaking always on the basis of comparative percentages, with single letters.

In terms of critical ratio, the greatest difference between the bright and the dull appears in the irrelevant column, where it amounts to 6.5 per cent with a critical ratio of 49.6. It is obvious that, with such high reliability, a very real difference exists between the bright and the dull in the number of wholly irrelevant spellings made. The second highest critical ratio, 20.9, appears in that class of errors designated as the substitution of a group of letters. Included in this class are errors in those groups of letters which, though they are wholly irrelevant, have not so vitally affected the word as to make it unrecognizable, and thus make it necessary to place the word in the wholly irrelevant column. The next greatest difference appears in the substitution of an actual word for the word dictated. The dull appear to be quite at sea in some substitutions. If the word *picture* is given, it is not at all unusual for the dull child to react by writing the word *boat.*

While the three largest differences appear as errors of substitution, the fourth most reliable difference, with a critical ratio of 16.7, is the omission of an entire group of letters. In this tendency tho dull soom to bo unablo to oatoh the rhythm of the word; as a result, they omit a syllable or some other group of letters. The

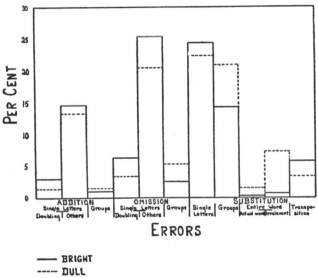

ERRORS

—— BRIGHT
---- DULL

Fig. 2. A Comparative Analysis of Kinds of Errors

greater percentage of errors in the next six groups appears on the bright pupils' side of the ledger. It will not be necessary to take up each of these errors in turn, but it is rather interesting to note that the bright children seem to have considerable difficulty with doubles, and tend to make a greater number of errors of transposition than do the dull children. The psychology of these errors will be taken up in the concluding chapter. (See Figure 2 for a graphic presentation of the degree of difference in the kinds of errors made.)

IRRELEVANT ERRORS ELIMINATED

Since there were so many wholly irrelevant misspellings, a question arose concerning what would happen to the percentage distribution if the wholly irrelevant efforts were eliminated. Such an elimination was effected and a new percentage distribution was made. (See Table IV.)

TABLE IV

A COMPARATIVE ANALYSIS OF NUMBER AND KINDS OF ERRORS WITH ALL WHOLLY IRRELEVANT MISSPELLINGS OMITTED

CLASSIFICATION		BRIGHT	DULL	DIFFERENCE
No. of Subjects		100	100	
Mean IQ		124.9 ±1.09	92.0 ±.87	−32.9 ±1.40
σ		16.3	12.9	
Words Omitted { Child Absent		150	671	+521
Spelling Not Attempted ..		45	423	+378
Total Words Spelled { No.		31,615	28,939	−2,676
% Correct		81.2 ±.148	42.7 ±.196	−38.5 ±.246
% Incorrect		18.8 ±.148	57.3 ±.196	+38.5 ±.246
% of Errors of Addition { Single Letters { Doubling		3.0 ±.137	1.5 ±.054	− 1.5 ±.147
Others ..		14.8 ±.285	14.0 ±.154	− 0.8 ±.324
Groups ..`...........		1.0 ±.080	1.5 ±.054	+ 0.5 ±.097
% of Errors of Omission { Single Letters { Doubling		6.2 ±.193	3.6 ±.083	− 2.6 ±.211
Others ..		26.8 ±.355	22.2 ±.185	− 4.6 ±.400
Groups		2.6 ±.127	5.6 ±.102	+ 3.0 ±.163
% of Errors of Substitution { Single Letters		24.8 ±.346	23.9 ±.189	− 0.9 ±.394
Groups		14.3 ±.280	22.4 ±.185	+ 8.1 ±.336
Another Actual Word		0.6 ±.006	1.6 ±.056	+ 1.0 ±.056
Transposition		5.9 ±.188	3.5 ±.081	− 2.4 ±.205
Total No. of Errors		7,086	23,065	+15,979

It is interesting to note that approximately the same differences exist in practically all of the classes of errors utilized in this study. Differences from the first results which might be considered significant appear in the following errors:

1. The addition of a single letter which is not one of a double.
2. The omission of a single letter which is not one of a double.

3. The substitution of a single letter.

4. The substitution of groups of letters.

These differences, however, were not large, varying from 0.7 per cent to 1.3 per cent. In no case was the sign wiped out; that is, dispensing with the class of irrelevant misspellings does not in any instance reverse the relative positions of bright and dull children with respect to the percentage of errors in the ten classes of errors remaining.

COMPARISON BETWEEN THE TEN BRIGHTEST AND THE TEN DULLEST
CHILDREN FROM EACH GRADE

Earlier, it was stated that this study was primarily concerned with a real educational problem, namely, the differences existing between differentiated classes in their ability to generalize in spelling. It was pointed out that while the bright group was really very superior, the dull group, with a mean IQ of 92.0 was not actually dull. In order to deal with a more theoretical problem, that of the differences between the bright and dull as measured by intelligence tests rather than as grouped by the intelligence quotient plus other criteria, the ten highest and the ten lowest IQ's were chosen from the three grades, IV A, IV B, and V B.

This reclassification also served as a check on a possible flaw in the division of the bright and dull in the main groups, where the number of each type was unequal in two of the three grades —IV B and V B—though the totals were exactly equated at 100. This inequality meant that an identical opportunity to make certain types of errors was not furnished the two groups. The difference, however, was very slight, and any objection to the method used is eliminated in the present grouping, where the number of children and the number and kinds of words are identically equated.

With the greater difference that existed between the mean IQ's of the two groups—for in this case the mean of the bright group is 137.8 and that of the dull 78.7—it might be expected that there would be a greater divergence in both the number and the kinds of errors made. This is exactly what happened, and the fact bears out the theory that the kinds of spelling errors made by children depend to some extent upon their intelligence. (See Table V.)

TABLE V

A COMPARATIVE ANALYSIS OF THE NUMBER AND KINDS OF ERRORS MADE BY
THE TEN BRIGHTEST AND THE TEN DULLEST CHILDREN OF EACH GRADE

CLASSIFICATION		BRIGHT	DULL	DIFFERENCE
No. of Subjects		30	30	
Mean IQ		137.8 ±1.785	78.7 ±.799	−59.1 ±1.958
σ		14.5	6.5	
Words Omitted {	Child Absent	0	121	+121
	Spelling Not Attempted ..	13	227	+214
Total Words Spelled {	No.	9,547	9,333	−214
	% Correct	84.4 ±.250	34.0 ±.330	−50.4 ±.414
	% Incorrect	15.6 ±.250	66.0 ±.330	+50.4 ±.414
% of Errors of Addition {	Single Letters { Doubling	3.5 ±.298	1.3 ±.084	− 2.2 ±.310
	Single Letters { Others ..	13.1 ±.548	13.4 ±.252	+ 0.3 ±.603
	Groups..............	0.8 ±.144	1.9 ±.101	+ 1.1 ±.176
% of Errors of Omission {	Single Letters { Doubling	6.7 ±.406	2.6 ±.117	− 4.1 ±.423
	Single Letters { Others ..	26.8 ±.719	20.3 ±.297	− 6.5 ±.778
	Groups	2.9 ±.272	5.8 ±.173	+ 2.9 ±.322
% of Errors of Substitution {	Single Letters	25.0 ±.703	21.9 ±.305	− 3.1 ±.766
	Groups	13.1 ±.548	21.5 ±.303	+ 8.4 ±.626
	Entire Word { Actual Word	0.8 ±.144	1.4 ±.087	+ 0.6 ±.168
	Entire Word { Irrelevant ..	1.1 ±.169	6.6 ±.183	+ 5.5 ±.249
	Transposition	6.1 ±.388	3.2 ±.130	− 2.9 ±.409
Total No. of Errors		1,726	8,321	+6,595

As far as the number of words misspelled is concerned, it will
be noticed that the difference between the total number of those
misspelled by the thirty brightest children and the total misspelled
by the thirty dullest children is 10 per cent greater than the
difference between the misspellings of the two main groups, where
a smaller spread between the mean IQ's existed. That difference,
however, would be expected. What is of greater significance is
the fact that in eight of the eleven classes of errors the difference
between the bright and the dull is intensified. Only in the addition of a single letter, which is not a double, the substitution of
an entire actual word, and the substitution of a wholly irrelevant
word, is there a decrease of the span between the percentages.
Close examination of Table V will reveal the fact that the differ-

ences between the two groups are increased anywhere from .03 per cent to 1.6 per cent. These differences are not very great, to be sure, but they are large enough to be significant. It is rather difficult to understand the unexpected change in the class of errors designated as "Addition of a single letter." Not only is there an alteration in this case of 1.8 per cent, but the sign is reversed, the thirty dullest children making more errors than the thirty brightest ones, while, when the two main groups were being considered, the bright group made more of this type of errors than the dull group. The differences in the other two classes of errors mentioned are not so great and can be accounted for in part by the greater probable error.

It was not thought advisable or necessary to work out the distribution within the eleven types of errors. However, since the most significant difference between the two groups has consistently been found to be in the number of irrelevant errors made, a table was drawn up showing the distribution of this kind of mistake. (See Table VI.)

TABLE VI

DISTRIBUTION OF PERCENTAGES OF IRRELEVANT ERRORS
OF THE TEN BRIGHTEST AND THE TEN DULLEST CHIL-
DREN OF EACH GRADE

	BRIGHT	DULL
N	7	27
M	$2.2 \pm .331$	9.6 ± 1.759
σ	1.3	13.55
Range	0.0–5.3	0.0–68.5

It will be noted that all except three of the thirty dull children made one or more irrelevant errors, while only seven of the bright children erred in this respect. The difference between the means is very marked.

WORDS ON CHILDREN'S GRADE LEVEL

Realizing that objections might be made to the findings of this study on the grounds that the results would have been quite different had words on the children's own grade level been given,

Generalization of Bright and Dull Children

TABLE

A COMPARATIVE ANALYSIS OF NUMBER AND KINDS OF ERRORS FROM WORDS ON

SUBJECTS	No. OF SUB-JECTS	MEAN IQ	σ	WORDS OMITTED		TOTAL WORDS SPELLED		
				Child Absent	Spelling Not At-tempted	No.	% Correct	% In-correct
BRIGHT								
One year advance	30	125.5	13.3	50	2	9,508	87.0	13.0
Grade level	30	125.5	13.3	0	1	2,999	94.4	5.6
Difference				−50	− 1	− 6,509	+ 7.4	− 7.4
DULL								
One year advance	30	93.6	12.9	0	30	9,530	38.3	61.7
Grade level	30	93.6	12.9	0	7	2.993	55.8	44.2
Difference				0	−23	− 6,537	+17.5	−17.5
TOTAL								
One year advance	60	109.6 ± 2.30	23.4	50	32	19,038	62.6 ± .237	37.4 ± .237
Grade level	60	109.6 ± 2.30	23.4	0	8	5,992	75.1 ± .377	24.9 ± .377
Difference				−50	−24	−13,046	+12.5 ± .445	−12.5 ± .445

− = Grade level less.   + = Grade level more.

it was decided, as has been previously explained, to give a sample of 100 words selected from those of their own grade level to ten children chosen at random from each of the six sections of pupils studied. The resulting 6,000 words spelled were treated in the same way as were those of the main group. The results indicate that children, in the main, will make the same kinds of errors in spelling words of their own grade level as they make in spelling words a year in advance of their present status. (See Table VII.)

It will be seen from Table VII that, as might of course be expected, the children had less difficulty with words of their own grade level than they did with words which were one year in advance of them. The bright group, for example, misspelled but 196 words of their own grade level out of 6,000 attempted. The dull, on the other hand, while showing an improvement over their

VII

SUBJECTS' GRADE LEVEL AND IN WORDS GIVEN ONE YEAR IN ADVANCE

% OF ERRORS OF ADDITION			% OF ERRORS OF OMISSION			% OF ERRORS OF SUBSTITUTION					TOTAL No. OF ERRORS
Single Letters		Groups	Single Letters		Groups	Single Letters	Groups	Entire Word		Transposition	
Doubling	Others		Doubling	Others				Actual Word	Irrelevant		
4.2	14.6	1.4	7.2	28.4	2.4	23.3	13.4	0.6	0.5	4.4	1,453
4.6	15.5	0.0	17.0	15.5	1.5	29.1	8.2	0.5	0.5	8.2	196
+0.4	+0.9	−1.4	+9.8	−12.9	−0.9	+5.8	−5.2	−0.1	0.0	+3.8	−1,257
1.3	13.1	1.9	3.6	21.6	5.3	22.5	21.7	0.8	5.1	3.1	8,093
1.6	14.3	1.4	4.6	23.7	4.3	21.1	21.2	0.9	2.1	4.7	1,736
+0.3	+1.2	−0.5	+1.0	+ 2.1	−1.0	−1.4	−0.5	+0.1	−3.0	+1.6	−6,357
1.8	13.3	1.8	4.1	22.6	4.8	22.6	20.4	0.8	4.4	3.3	9,546
± .092	± .235	± .092	± .137	± .289	± .148	± .289	± .278	± .062	± .142	± .123	
1.9	14.4	1.3	5.9	23.0	4.1	21.9	19.9	0.9	2.0	5.1	1,932
± .210	± .539	± .174	± .361	± .645	± .304	± .635	± .612	± .145	± .214	± .338	
+0.1	+1.1	−0.5	+1.8	+ 0.4	−0.7	−0.7	−0.5	+0.1	−2.4	+1.8	−7,614
± .229	± .588	± .197	± .386	± .707	± .335	± .698	± .672	± .158	± .257	± .360	

work on the words which were one year in advance, misspelled nearly one-half of the words of their own grade level.

Upon analyzing the misspelled words, it was found that in eight of the eleven classes there were no significant differences— accepting a critical ratio of three as indicatory of a significant difference—between the percentage of the various kinds of errors made in spelling words given one year in advance and those made in spelling words chosen from the child's own grade level. Only in the omission of a single letter which was one of a double, in the substitution of an entirely irrelevant word, and in transposition was there a critical ratio greater than three. In two of these three types of errors, namely the omission of the second of a double and the transposing of letters, the critical ratios were 4.7 and 5.0 respectively—not strikingly large, though important ratios.

A very great difference, however, was found in the percentage of irrelevant errors made, the critical ratio going to 9.3. This can undoubtedly be explained by the fact that the children, bright and dull alike, would not be so likely to be completely baffled by a word of their own grade level as by a word one year in advance. On the whole, words of their own grade level would be less unfamiliar to them. It should be kept in mind, however, that in spelling even the words of their own grade level the dull still make more than four times as great a percentage of irrelevant errors as do the bright.

SUMMARY

Briefly summarizing the findings set forth in this chapter the following conclusions are evident.

1. Marked differences in degree exist between the bright and the dull, in the kind as well as in the number of errors made.

2. These differences were but little affected when the wholly irrelevant misspellings were discarded.

3. An analysis of the errors made by the ten brightest and those made by the ten dullest children in each grade results in an even greater gap between the percentages of the types of errors made by the bright and the dull.

4. The children made very much the same kinds of errors on words chosen from their own grade level as they did on words chosen from those ordinarily taught one year in advance of their present grade status.

CHAPTER VI

RESULTS: WORD AND SYLLABLE PLACEMENT OF ERRORS

Analysis of the word and syllable placement of errors failed to yield such clear-cut results as grew out of the other two lines of approach to the problem of this study. It was found that although the dull children misspell a great many more one-syllable words than the bright misspell, they also misspell a great many more two-, three-, and four-syllable words. The differences, too, in the syllable placement of the error are not pronounced, though in many cases they are statistically significant. A glance at Figure 3 will show how closely the curves of the two classes of children resemble each other in form. Each group finds the middle of the word the most difficult to spell, the end of the word second in difficulty, and the beginning of the word the easiest to spell; and each group finds that the length of the word increases the difficulty.

EFFECT OF SYLLABLE LENGTH OF WORD

Although Figure 3 indicates that there is some difference between the two groups with respect to the placement of errors, it does not show exactly how great those differences are. In order to discover these facts, the following attack on the raw data was made. The ten brightest children from each of the bright sections and the ten dullest children from each of the dull sections were separated from the main groups. In cases where a member of the selected group had missed a block of words through absence, he was eliminated and the child having the IQ next in order was substituted. All words which a child did not attempt to spell were included among the misspellings. These two precautions were taken in order that the total number of one-, two-, three-, and four-syllable words should be equivalent, respectively, for each intelligence group.

Now it became possible to consider on a percentage basis the misspellings only. That is, the total number of misspelled words of the different syllable lengths was found. On this base, the degree of difficulty in terms of percentage was worked out for each of the four word lengths considered. (See Table VIII.) Since the

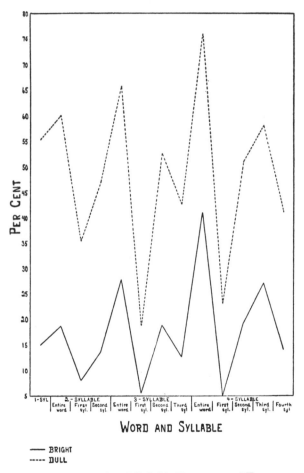

WORD AND SYLLABLE

—— BRIGHT
----- DULL

FIG. 3.   Word and Syllable Frequency of Errors

two groups were exactly equated with respect to the number of subjects spelling them and the number and types of words dictated, the differences between the difficulty-percentages indicate clearly the differences between the bright and dull children.

TABLE VIII

COMPARATIVE PERCENTAGES OF MISSPELLINGS ON BASIS OF SYLLABLE LENGTH
OF WORD BY THE TEN BRIGHTEST AND THE TEN DULLEST
CHILDREN FROM EACH GRADE

	BRIGHT	DULL	DIFFERENCE
Number	30	30	
Mean IQ	137.8 ± 1.785	80.3 ± .591	− 57.5 ± 1.880
σ	14.5	4.8	
One-Syllable Words	25.1 ± .755	27.3 ± .371	+ 2.2 ± .841
Two-Syllable Words	49.9 ± .843	54.2 ± .418	+ 4.3 ± .941
Three-Syllable Words	19.6 ± .688	15.6 ± .303	− 4.0 ± .752
Four-Syllable Words	5.6 ± .310	2.9 + .141	− 2.7 ± .341

Table VIII shows that the dull had greater difficulty than the bright, speaking in terms of percentages, with the one- and two-syllable words, while the positions of the two groups were reversed in respect to the three- and four-syllable words. The difference existing with respect to one-syllable words is not a significant one, representing a critical ratio of but 2.6. The bright, however, do have a significant advantage over the dull in the spelling of two-syllable words. The difference is 4.3, with a critical ratio of 4.6. In the spelling of three-syllable words there is a difference of still greater reliability, and in this type of words the dull exceed the bright. The greatest difference, in terms of the critical ratio which is 7.9, exists in the difficulty found by children in spelling four-syllable words. It is rather surprising to note that again the dull excel the bright, the former making only slightly more than one-half as high a percentage of errors as the latter. These findings are not so inconsistent with preceding results as they at first appear to be. An explanation will be given in the final chapter.

SYLLABLE PLACEMENT OF ERRORS

Since the length of the word was found to have differing effects upon the bright and the dull, it was thought that possibly certain parts of words would prove more difficult for one group than for the other. Therefore, using the same sixty students who furnished the data concerning the comparative effect of word length on difficulty of spelling, their errors were analyzed from the point of view of syllable placement. (See Table IX.)

A significant difference exists between the bright and the dull in the relative difficulty of spelling the first and the second syllables of two-syllable words. The bright find the first syllable easier; the dull, the second. The "spread" of difficulty is much greater for the bright; that is, there is a difference of 29.0 per cent between the difficulty the bright find in spelling the first and the second syllables. The dull, on the other hand, present a difference of only 14.0 per cent.

Again, in the three-syllable words a difference in the degree of difficulty appears between the two groups as regards both the first and the second syllable. The percentages relative to the third syllable are almost identical. Once more, however, a greater range of differences is seen to exist between the difficulty of spelling the syllables in the case of the bright.

In the spelling of no syllable of the four-syllable words is there a statistically significant difference between the two groups. It was felt that this was due to the fact that the sampling of four-syllable words was so small that the high probable error wiped out whatever differences might have been present. In order to test this assumption, eighty-eight bright children and eighty-eight dull children were chosen from the main groups. Selections had to be made in order that the two groups might be exactly equated not only in number, but in grade and number and types of words spelled, as well. The increase of the total number of children from 60 to 176 resulted, of course, in a larger sampling of four-syllable words, and real differences were now found to exist between the two groups in spelling the first and the third syllables. But once more there appeared the pertinent fact that the span between the percentage of errors in spelling the different syllables was considerably greater with the bright than with the dull. (See Table X.)

TABLE IX

COMPARATIVE PERCENTAGES OF SYLLABLE PLACEMENT OF ERRORS MADE BY
THE TEN BRIGHTEST AND THE TEN DULLEST CHILDREN
FROM EACH GRADE

		BRIGHT	DULL	DIFFERENCE
Number		30	30	
Mean IQ		137.8 ± 1.785	80.3 ± .591	− 57.5 ± 1.880
σ		14.5	4.8	
Two-Syllable Words	1st Syl.	35.5 ± 1.093	43.0 ± .479	+ 7.5 ± 1.193
	2nd Syl.	64.5 ± 1.093	57.0 ± .479	− 7.5 ± 1.193
Three-Syllable Words	1st Syl.	14.2 ± 1.207	23.5 ± .540	+ 9.3 ± 1.322
	2nd Syl.	50.9 ± 1.727	41.4 ± .742	− 9.5 ± 1.880
	3rd Syl.	35.0 ± 1.835	34.9 ± .715	− 0.1 ± 1.973
Four-Syllable Words	1st Syl.	11.7 ± 1.885	15.6 ± 1.147	+ 3.9 ± 2.181
	2nd Syl.	29.9 ± 2.637	27.2 ± 1.410	− 2.7 ± 2.990
	3rd Syl.	38.0 ± 2.799	32.3 ± 1.477	− 5.7 ± 3.165
	4th Syl.	21.3 ± 2.361	25.3 ± 1.376	+ 4.0 ± 2.733

Briefly summarized, the data given in this discussion of the word and syllable placement of errors have yielded the following information.

1. In terms of comparative percentages, the dull have greater difficulty than the bright with one- and two-syllable words, while

TABLE X

COMPARATIVE ANALYSIS OF SYLLABLE PLACEMENT OF ERROR IN 656 FOUR-
SYLLABLE WORDS

SUBJECTS	No.	MEAN IQ	σ	1ST. SYL.	2ND. SYL.	3RD. SYL.	4TH. SYL.
Total							
Bright ...	88	128.6	15.5	8.5	29.7	41.1	21.0
		± 1.114		± .924	± 1.511	± 1.625	± 1.342
Dull	88	93.5	12.4	14.0	27.8	34.1	24.0
		± .892		± .695	± .897	± .951	± .857
Difference		−35.1		+ 5.5	− 1.9	− 7.0	+ 3.0
		± .1427		± 1.156	± 1.757	± 1.883	± 1.592

the situation is reversed with regard to three- and four-syllable words.

2. Generally speaking, the bright have less difficulty with the beginning of a word, more with the middle, and less with the end of a word than do the dull; their percentages also show a much greater range of difficulty between syllables.

CHAPTER VII

RESULTS: PHONETIC ANALYSIS

One of the primary aims of this investigation was to discover whether or not bright children make more phonetic transfer than the dull, in the spelling of unfamiliar words. No conclusions could be drawn with respect to correct spellings, although it might be logically deduced that since the bright are much more successful than the dull in spelling supposedly unfamiliar words, they are utilizing units of past experience; that is, they are making correct generalizations. However, that conclusion can only be assumed.

Though positive transfer can not be directly determined, it is possible, through a classification of the misspelled words, to learn the amount of negative transfer made. That is, if a child spells *house*, *h-o-u-s-e*, there is no way of discovering whether he has so spelled it because he has translated the phonetic qualities of the word into those letter counterparts which are correct in this instance, or whether he has previously learned to spell the word. If, however, he spells it *h-o-u-s*, it becomes at least comparatively certain that he is rendering it phonetically. Other bases of generalization have undoubtedly been at work. For example, the configuration of the misspelling is much the same as that of the original word. But the outstanding characteristic of the spelling is its phonetic correctness. The phonetic rendition has led the child into error, to be sure. Perhaps its results are more often faulty than correct. With that problem, as was previously stated, this investigation is not concerned. It should be kept in mind that the writer is measuring negative rather than positive transfer; but if, as Horn remarks, only a very naïve person would assume that simply because there is a positive transfer there is no negative transfer, so also may it be said that only a very naïve person would assume that because there is a negative transfer, there is no positive transfer. In other words, if it can be shown conclusively that children make negative phonetic transfer, it follows that they also make positive transfer, and if the dull make much

43

less negative transfer, they will probably tend also to make much less positive transfer.

All the misspelled words were divided, as was explained in Chapter III, into two groups—phonetic and non-phonetic. The results are very enlightening and furnish the outstanding conclusion of this study. (See Table XI.) An examination of Table

TABLE XI

A COMPARATIVE PHONETIC ANALYSIS

SUBJECTS	No. OF SUB-JECTS	MEAN IQ	σ	TOTAL WORDS SPELLED INCORRECTLY		
				No.	% Phonetic	% Non-phonetic
IV A						
Bright	36	126.4	8.8	2,473	68.9	31.1
Dull	36	88.5	9.8	7,724	37.8	62.2
Difference		−37.9		+ 5,251	−31.1	+31.1
IV B						
Bright	35	110.5	11.3	2,031	65.5	34.5
Dull	25	89.5	13.7	4,415	46.0	54.0
Difference		−21.0		+ 2,384	−19.5	+19.5
V B						
Bright	29	140.6	12.3	1,498	74.7	25.2
Dull	39	96.8	11.2	6,262	46.1	53.9
Difference		−43.8		+ 4,764	−28.6	+28.7
TOTAL						
Bright	100	124.9 ± 1.09	16.3	6,002	69.2 ± .401	30.8 ± .401
Dull	100	92.0 ± .87	12.9	18,401	42.6 ± .245	57.4 ± .245
Difference		−32.9 ± 1.40		+12,399	−26.6 ± .470	+26.6 ± .470

XI reveals the fact that while the bright erred on the phonetic side in 69.2 per cent of their misspelled words, the dull made such generalizations in only 42.6 per cent of the cases,—a difference of 26.6 per cent. When it is considered that the probable error of this difference is only .470, resulting in a critical ratio of 37, it becomes obvious that the bright and the dull differ sharply in their capacity to generalize phonetically. The bright have made a transfer in over two-thirds of their misspellings, while the dull saw identical elements in considerably less than half of theirs. Further examination of Table XI shows that the percentage of the phonetic misspellings decreases in the same order as does the mean IQ of each of the six sections; that is, when the six sections are arranged on an intelligence scale, the highest IQ group has the highest number of phonetic misspellings, the second highest IQ group, the second highest number of phonetic misspellings, and so on down the list in perfect correlation.

In order that this comparison might be carried a step further, the phonetic misspellings of the ten brightest and the ten dullest children from each grade were compared. If phonetic generalization is dependent upon intelligence, then these two selected groups, with a greater difference between their mean IQ's than the larger groups had, should show a wider variation between their comparative abilities in the matter of phonetic spelling. That was what happened. While in the two main groups there was a difference between the means of 32.9, in the smaller and selected groups there was a difference of 59.1. The difference between the percentage of phonetic misspellings increased from 26.6 in the main group to 34.6 in the selected groups. The thirty brightest children showed more ability than the main bright group, and the thirty dullest showed less ability than the main dull group. (See Table XII.)

TABLE XII

A COMPARATIVE PHONETIC ANALYSIS OF THE WORDS MISSPELLED BY THE TEN BRIGHTEST AND THE TEN DULLEST CHILDREN IN EACH GRADE

SUBJECTS	No. OF SUB-JECTS	MEAN IQ	σ	TOTAL WORDS SPELLED INCORRECTLY		
				Raw Score	% Phonetic	% Non-phonetic
Bright	30	137.8 + 1.785	14.5	1,491	71.0 + .792	29.0 + .792
Dull	30	78.7 ± .799	6.5	6,159	36.4 ± .413	63.6 ± .413
Difference		−59.1 ± 1.958		+4,668	−34.6 ± .893	+34.6 ± .893

A graphic presentation of the spread of the phonetic misspellings of these two selected groups appears in Figure 4. It will be noted that there is a wide difference not only between the means, but also between the extremes. They do not come even close to coinciding. Although there is some overlapping, it is very slight. Only seven of the bright children make as little phonetic transfer as the brightest of the dull. The remaining twenty-three children are superior. Given a somewhat wider difference between the mean IQ's, the overlapping would probably disappear altogether.

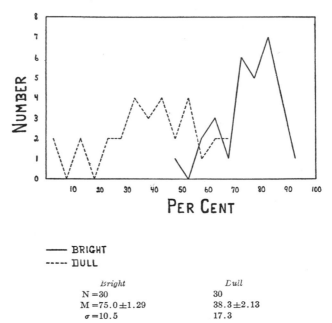

— BRIGHT
----- DULL

	Bright	*Dull*
N =	30	30
M =	75.0 ± 1.29	38.3 ± 2.13
σ =	10.5	17.3

FIG. 4.   Phonetic Misspellings by the Ten Brightest and the Ten Dullest
Children from Each Grade

In this phase of the experiment as well as in those previously discussed, a group containing a random selection of the children were given a sampling of words of their own grade level. The results are even more striking than those in the situations presented earlier. While the sixty subjects phonetically misspelled 48.1 per cent out of their total number of misspelled words when working with words one year in advance of their grade status, they phonetically misspelled 48.5 per cent of the words given on their own grade level—a difference of 0.4. (See Table XIII.) When it is observed that the probable error is 1.42, any actual difference disappears. Therefore it seems safe to conclude that, had the children been tested solely with words on their own grade level, the results growing out of this phase of the investigation would not have been in any way affected.

TABLE XIII

A COMPARATIVE PHONETIC ANALYSIS OF WORDS GIVEN ON SUBJECTS' GRADE LEVEL AND WORDS GIVEN ONE YEAR IN ADVANCE OF GRADE LEVEL

SUBJECTS	NO. OF SUBJECTS	MEAN IQ	σ	TOTAL WORDS SPELLED INCORRECTLY		
				Raw Score	% Phonetic	% Non-phonetic
One Year Advance	60	109.6 ± 2.30	23.4	7,113	48.1 ± .590	51.9 ± .590
Grade Level	60	109.6 ± 2.30	23.4	1,493	48.5 ± 1.290	51.5 ± 1.290
Difference				−5,620	+ 0.4 ± 1.42	− 0.4 ± 1.42

CHAPTER VIII

CONCLUSIONS AND IMPLICATIONS

The problem of discovering differences between bright and dull children in their ability to generalize in spelling was attacked in three different ways: (1) by means of an analysis of the kinds of errors made by them; (2) by means of determining the incidence of errors as related to length of word, and syllable placement; (3) by means of a phonetic-non-phonetic classification of the misspelled words. The interpretation of the findings presented in the three preceding chapters follows.

KINDS OF ERRORS

The results stated in Chapter V showed that in certain kinds of errors bright children excelled the dull, while in other kinds dull children excelled the bright. The interpretation of such differences must necessarily be largely speculative.

The bright, it was found, consistently have much greater difficulty with single letters. (It should be kept in mind that all these comparisons are made on the basis of percentages. In no type of error did the bright exceed the dull in the raw score.) This difficulty may be due to the fact that single letters offer greater possibilities for phonetic renderings than do groups of letters. That is, a child capable of a high degree of generalizing is more likely to spell *jolly*, *g-o-l-y*, than he is to spell it *p-l-e-d-l*. (If the second rendition seems too far-fetched to be credible, a review of the irrelevant misspellings in Chapter IV will settle all doubts on this score.) In the first misspelling, the child has made two single-letter errors, each of which is phonetic. Probably similar phonetic generalizations account, then, for the preponderance of single-letter errors made by the bright, for it will be remembered that 69.2 per cent of all the words misspelled by the bright are phonetic translations, while only 42.6 per cent of the dull misspellings are phonetic.

Single letter errors accounted for six of the eleven types of errors

48

in the classification used. The remaining five were mistakes involving groups of letters, in each of which type of error the dull excelled the bright. The explanation of these facts seems to be the one just offered relative to single letter errors; in this case, the dull, failing to make phonetic renditions of the words given them, add, omit, or substitute groups of letters which, in the great majority of cases, have little if any association with the sound qualities of the word. Thus to spell *table*, *t-x-m-b-l-e*, shows a lack of ability to translate the sound of long *a*.

It will not be necessary to give a detailed interpretation of the differences found in each of the eleven types of errors utilized. They have been treated in general in the above discussion. Some of the outstanding variations, however, may well be considered briefly.

This investigation shows that the bright child is twice as likely as the dull child to make the error of doubling a letter. For example, he may spell *advise*, *a-d-d-v-i-s-e*. An excellent phonetic transfer! He is given two sounds to translate into letters, and he errs in spelling the sound *ad*, *a-d-d*.

The same situation exists in a second type of error in which the bright child makes a greater percentage of errors than the dull child; namely, omitting the second letter of a double. When he spells *rabbit*, *r-a-b-i-t*, it is obvious that he is not violating the principles of good phonetic generalization procedure. Though he has omitted the second *b*, the word sounds satisfactory. If the child had gone further and broken the word up into its two pronunciation units, perhaps the mistake would not have been made. Evidently he failed to make this last type of motor transfer.

A large difference was found between bright and dull children in the number of errors of transposition made, the bright exceeding the dull by a considerable amount. Perhaps here, as in the preceding instances, the explanation lies in the fact that the bright generalize phonetically more than the dull. Such a word as *scheme*, for example, might easily be rendered phonetically as *s-c-h-e-e-m*. The child who so spells it has transposed the *m* and the *e*, but he has given a phonetic spelling, nevertheless. To check up on this supposition, the investigator classified in phonetic and non-phonetic groups 300 transposition errors chosen at random from the bright children's list. Of these 191 proved to be phonetic and 109 non-phonetic errors. On classifying the same number of dull children's errors of this type, it was found that 164 were phonetic and 136 non-phonetic.

This difference represents a difference in raw scores of 27 points —not quite so great as was expected. Evidently errors of transposition have a tendency to be phonetic when made by either bright or dull children, although the bright have an advantage in this respect.

While the dull group excelled the bright in none of the single-letter errors, they did so in every one of the five group-errors. Noticeable among these last errors was that of substituting a wholly irrelevant spelling, such as *rszilm*, for the word, *defeated*. In this kind of misspelling, the dull had a percentage of error more than nine times as great as the bright. The psychological explanation appears to lie in the inability of the dull to adjust themselves to a new situation, to meet it by drawing more or less heavily upon past experiences. Such wholly irrelevant spellings are illogical; the child has failed to recognize in the word a single element identical with some element in his past spelling experience. The visual appearance of the irrelevant word is markedly, if not wholly, different from the one dictated; the pronunciation units have been completely lost, and no phonetic transfer whatever has been made in spelling it. This type of error represents the best example in spelling of an almost total lack of ability to generalize. It is important to remember that it is an error which the dull child is far more likely to make than the bright one. The bright child does not fall into such a widespread and illogical error because he is too much on the alert for transfer possibilities. As has been pointed out earlier, in over two-thirds of the cases he succeeds in making a phonetic translation of the word given him, even though that phonetic translation results in an incorrect spelling. It follows that a phonetic translation cannot at the same time be irrelevant.

The remaining four types of errors, involving groups of letters in which the dull children excel the bright ones have a somewhat similar psychological background. A wide difference, for example, exists between the two classes of children in the matter of substituting one group of letters for another. Included in this class of errors is the substitution of an irrelevant group of letters—

a group, however, that is not large enough to cause the word to be placed in the wholly irrelevant-word column. Again, in making this type of error, the dull show an inability to generalize. For example, if a child spells *monument, m-o-n-s-l-i-g-h-s,* he has substituted a group of irrelevant letters for that part of the word which should have been spelled *ument.* There appears to be no logic behind such a substitution. Perhaps some slight signs of visual transfer might be discovered in respect to the length of the word, but the pronunciation units have been entirely lost, and there is not a hint of phonetic transfer. In the light of these facts it becomes significant that the bright children are much less likely than the dull to make this kind of error.

In conclusion, it appears that phonetic generalization is the dominating factor in the psychology of the differences in kinds of spelling errors made by bright and dull children. The bright child, possessing a high degree of ability in translating sounds into letters, makes those mistakes which would quite naturally result from the varied phonetic qualities of the English language; while the dull child, less capable of adapting himself to a new situation, makes those errors which have little if any phonetic foundation.

WORD LENGTH AND SYLLABLE PLACEMENT

According to the findings presented in Chapter VI, significant differences exist between the bright and the dull in their ability to spell words of varying syllable length. The bright, it was found, have less difficulty with two-syllable words, and more difficulty with three- and four-syllable words. At first glance this would seem to be a rather surprising conclusion, for it might be supposed that the longer and more complicated the word the more likely the dull children would be to misspell it. Such is indeed the case—but the bright children are still more likely to do so.

The psychological explanation of this situation appears to be that it springs from the same source that was found to be at the root of the differences in kinds of errors; namely, phonetic generalization. The longer the word, the more opportunity for negative phonetic transfer. Assuming that the dull child has a tendency to learn to spell by rote, it follows that he is not so prone to be as seriously affected by the length of the word as is the bright child, who depends more upon his ability to generalize. The dull child knows the word or he does not know it. The bright child, on the other hand, if faced with the problem of spelling a one- or two-syllable word with which he is unfamiliar, stands a fairly good chance of hitting upon the correct phonetic translation. When, however, the word to be spelled is made up of three or four syllables, the opportunity for him to go astray phonetically is considerably greater. Hence, comparatively speaking, he finds the increase in difficulty of the longer words over the shorter ones somewhat greater than does the dull child.

The above line of reasoning is borne out to some extent by the findings with respect to the syllable placement of the error. As was stated in Chapter VI, it was found that the bright have a smaller percentage of difficulty with the beginning of the word and a greater difficulty with the middle and the end of the word. The result of this is that the percentages of errors made by the bright also show a much wider range between those of the first and those of the last syllables of a word than do the percentages of the dull. The rather obvious conclusion to be drawn is that when the dull miss a word they are more likely than the bright to miss the whole thing; that is, if it is a three-syllable word, they are likely to err in all three syllables. The bright, on the other hand, show a different distribution of mistakes. In their attempt to spell a word phonetically, they may err in spelling a single syllable but not in spelling every one. Hence, the greater "spread" of their errors. As an example, take the word *government*. The bright child, spelling the word *g-o-v-i-r-n-m-e-n-t*, errs only in the second syllable; the dull child, spelling it *g-e-v-e-m-n-o-s-t*, errs in all three. His non-phonetic rendering has resulted in an even distribution of errors.

PHONETIC ANALYSIS

So much time has already been given to a consideration of the comparative ability of the bright and the dull to generalize phonetically, that the main finding of this investigation comes somewhat as an anti-climax. The data resulting from the classification of all misspelled words in phonetic and non-phonetic groups have been presented in the preceding chapter, and need but little interpretation. Given the same words, a group of bright children will come much nearer to making phonetic translations than will a group of dull children. The reason for this trend evidently lies in the fact that the bright child possesses greater ability in recognizing phonetic elements in the new word which are identical with those which he has previously used. He is asked to spell the unfamiliar word *conductor*. Immediately he recognizes certain sounds, such as *on* and *or*. He remembers, perhaps, that the *on* sound was spelled *o-n* in *conduct*, and the *or* sound, *e-r*, in *order*. He succeeds in making a positive transfer of the sound *on*, but spells the *or*, *e-r*. The latter transfer is correct phonetically, but negative, nevertheless. Hence though he has spelled his word incorrectly, he has generalized soundly. The dull child, it was found in Chapter V, is more likely to make an error involving, not a single letter, but a group of letters; so he may spell the word *condimslur*, which is, of course, non-phonetic. Such appears to be the explanation of the situation found when the data were treated from this point of view.

EDUCATIONAL IMPLICATIONS

The thesis that intelligence is an important factor of generalization in spelling is borne out by this experiment. Whether or not the same condition exists in other school studies is not definitely known. If, as Gates says, intelligence is generalization—the same idea is advanced by Thorndike in his study of *Mental Discipline in High School Studies*—then it follows that bright children will generalize to a greater extent than dull children in every situation. Such being the case, it seems that the method of procedure used with differentiated classes should be affected. If the bright child generalizes so much more than the dull, then he should be given the opportunity to utilize that ability to the utmost. It must be kept in mind, however, that the dull child also makes many perfectly good transfers. The difference is not in kind but in degree. It cannot be said that the bright generalize and the dull do not. Although the dull should not be barred from training in generalization, it appears to the writer that they need, in spelling, much more specific work with the letter and syllable structure of the word. This suggestion grows out of the finding that the dull have a comparatively high incidence of error with respect to groups of letters.

A more specific educational implication than the one discussed in the preceding paragraph rises out of the kinds of errors the two groups make. While it must be constantly kept in mind that neither group is wholly free of any one of the eleven classes of errors, differences in the degree of freedom from these errors are considerable, and should receive the attention of teachers of spelling. For example, since it is known that a bright section of pupils will have a high percentage, comparatively speaking, of errors of transposition, more attention should be given in that bright section than in a dull section to the eradication of such errors. The same principle holds true of the error of faulty doubling of a letter, and that of omitting the second letter of a double. On the other hand, since the dull sections have a tendency to add, omit, or substitute groups of letters, manifesting a difficulty in appreciating the syllable structure and the rhythm of the word, they should be given more training than the bright in breaking the word up into parts, in seeing how it goes together. But always such differentiated training ought to be determined by the degree of training needed—of deciding where the emphasis shall be placed.

SUMMARY

Briefly summed up, this investigation comes to the following conclusions:

1. Bright and dull children show marked differences of degree in the kinds of spelling errors which they make.

   a. The bright make a higher percentage of one-letter errors.

   b. The dull make a higher percentage of group-errors.

2. Bright and dull children are affected differently by the length of the word and by the position of the syllable.

   a. The bright have a lower percentage of difficulty with the shorter words and a higher percentage of difficulty with the longer words, than the dull.

   b. The bright have a lower percentage of difficulty with the first part of the word and a higher one with the middle and last parts.

3. The bright are much more likely than the dull to spell words phonetically.

4. The psychological explanation of each of these differences appears to lie in the marked superiority of the bright over the dull in phonetic generalization ability.